The Most Comprehensive Self-Discovery Book Ever!

The Most Comprehensive Self-Discovery Book Ever!

Table Of Contents

Foreword

Learning the way we work (as well as other people) is a very important aspect when it comes to living an effective life.

We were created unique and though we are like other people, we are also unlike other people. If we were just like everyone else, then everyone will be a carbon copy of one another with no individuality or artistic sense. Mankind will be boring – even monkeys and other animals have different species which evidences diversity.

You and I are diverse, unlike one another. We cannot be like others – we can only be ourselves.

But do not just be content with being yourself – be a better you!

That is why the Enneagram of Personality is such an important subject to undertake.

With the diversity of mankind, it is more important to learn how to understand other people and understand how they work. Don't try and change yourself to fit into their mold nor try and change them to fit ours – it is not what we are called to do.

This book is a culmination of years of study, analysis of human psychology and personal experience rolled together.

What works for one may not work for another and likewise you may or may not agree with some of the results whether it is pertaining to you current predicament or not – it is just for self-discovering purposes with no intention to offend nor ridicule.

There is no right or wrong type.

Please do not get worked up when your result appears because life is a process of discovery and a constant journey. You might be different 10 years down the line... you will never know.

Besides, if anything else matters... know that living an effective life involves interactions with other people which is often really difficult because we do not understand them.

Suffice to know for now, that reading this book will open your mind if you let it – take notes if necessary and above all, have fun with it!

Get ready to unlock the mystery and your true potential at the same time!

The Most In Depth Self Discovery Book - Ever!

Go Deep In Understanding Yourself To The Core And Seeking Your Origins

Chapter 1:

The Basics

Synopsis

Enneagrams are a fascinating tool. Discover its humble origins, its role in psychology and how it helps people.

This chapter talks about:

- ➢ The origins of enneagrams

- ➢ Who started it and how it has evolved

- ➢ Why it is important for understanding others

- ➢ Its popularity in personal development circles

- ➢ What are the 9 different types – reformer, helper, achiever, individualist, investigator, loyalist, enthusiast, challenger and peacemaker.

Personal development as you know it will change once you discover your type. Read on to find the beauty in every different type!

Where To Start

The Enneagram is typically known for its accuracy in predicting the various types of human personality. The first inception of the enneagram begun with George Ivanovich Gurdjieff – an Armenian mystic and spiritual teacher. Although the enneagram model has been known since ancient times, it was Gurdjieff who make the model publicly known.

Only in recent decades that the enneagram gained more prominence in the field of personal developmental studies through these two individuals – Oscar Ichazo and Claudio Naranjo.

It is not really a typology that is perpetuated among academic circles – especially in the field of psychology. However, it has a strong following among personal development circles because of its unique structure for finding out how people work.

Simply put, if you do not know yourself, it is very hard to begin understanding others.

Once you know yourself, you will be able to do some guesswork on how other people work, hence saving you a lot of frustration when dealing with people who are from different 'types'.

The test is fairly accurate if the person taking the test answers them authentically.

The enneagram consist of 9 different points, each point is connected to another point in a form of connectivity and association. Each point also affects the adjacent point which you will learn in the chapters to follow.

Below is a diagram of the chart and how you can understand the differences between all the different types and their placements. In the next chapter, you will learn how you can take a few tests and see how they work together to discover your type as well as a sub-type.

The exciting part of self discovery is about to begin! Which of the 9 types will you be?

This chapter talks about:

- Websites where you can take the test

- Where your type is and how it is affected by the one adjacent to it and connected to it by the lines

- The effect of 'wings'...

- What are sub-types?

- All the different combinations of types and sub-types added together to form your unique personality

In order to live an effective life, understanding your fixations, ego, holy ideas, temptations and other factors your type tends to lean towards – it is important to know them deep down, otherwise you will not be able to live true to yourself.

The Different Consciousness Levels

First of all, please take the test from either one of these 3 sources:

http://www.eclecticenergies.com/enneagram/test.php

http://www.enneagraminstitute.com/begin.asp

http://similarminds.com/test.html

After taking all some (or all) of these tests, you'll discover how you can easily identify 2 things:

(1) You will know which of the 9 'types' you are. You will be named among one of these types:

- The Reformer
- The Helper
- The Achiever
- The Individualist
- The Investigator
- The Loyalist

- The Enthusiast

- The Challenger

- The Peacemaker

(2)   Note that among these 9 types, there is always a possibility that you could be leaning 'left' or 'right' towards one of the other accompanying types. In other words, you could be a *pure* achiever, an achiever with a helper 'wing', or an achiever with an individualistic 'wing'.

(3)   Each type is also mildly affected by other types they are connected with (See the diagram again for a better idea)

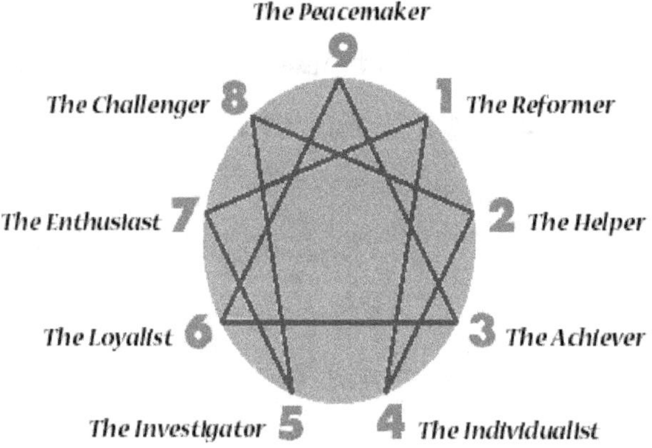

For example, a helper will feel stressed when a challenger is around but at ease when 'helping' an individualist. Likewise Loyalists are stressed around achievers but comfortable with peacemakers. This adds further environmental dynamics to all the types involved.

(4)   There's also one more component called a subtype. It is also called an instinctual energy by some. What this means is, along with their type, a natural sub-type exist for all people and this instinctual level manifests itself it 3 forms:

- Self-preservation
- Sexual
- Social

Self-preservation sub-types are people who may internally place emphasis and externally express the need to protect themselves. The sexual sub-types (not sexual bodily...) are more to intimacy and forming close bonds with their partners and the social sub-types are typically those who function at their best when in large groups.

At the end of the day, with the 9 types and 3 sub-types, you will typically end up with at least 27 combinations (not including the various wings and stress points).

Remember that when you take the test, you must remain calm, collected and not under stress. Do not ponder on the answers for too long – if you take too long, you are over analytical and your answers will be marred by your biasness. Do not answer socially acceptable or idealistic answers either – do understand that one type is not superior or inferior to the other... the key point is to understand who you are and be yourself – a better you but not a different you.

Let's go into detail about each type and how to deal with each of them!

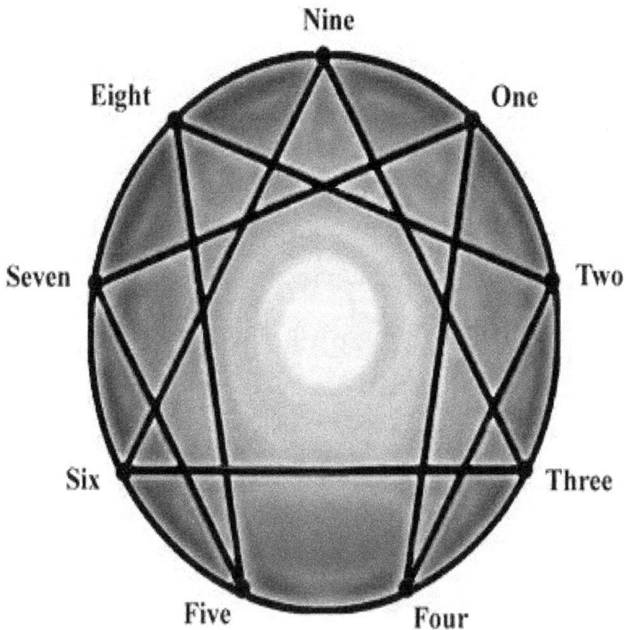

Chapter 2:

The Reformer and The Helper

Synopsis

The 'Martin Luther' of today, reformers are typically people who seek to change things and build upon the imperfections to make things more perfect.

This chapter talks about:

- ➢ What a reformer is all about

- ➢ Why are reformers good to have around

- ➢ What is most difficult about reformers

- ➢ Dealing with them and bringing out the best

- ➢ Who they get along with

- ➢ Who they don't along with

Championing the cause of change, whether for the better or worse is part and parcel of a reformer – learn to love them, accept them for who they are and bring the best out of them!

You can always count on them to lend a helping hand. These people live to serve and they enjoy doing it in the process!

This chapter talks about:

> What a helper is all about

> Why are helper good to have around

> What is most difficult about helpers

> Dealing with them and bringing out the best

> Who they get along with

> Who they don't along with

Living in service and contribution to others is the core structure of a helper – learn to accept them, understand them for who they are and bring the best out of them!

The First Two

The reformers are the perfectionists of self, home and society. Their constant desire is to improve things, make things better because things always never seem good enough to them. Their attention to detail is impeccable – often finding fault and fixing even the smallest things.

Highly principled and never compromising, they live by the book and follow all the rules – they even expect others to do so as well. They also tend to be ambitious and to a point, like a workaholic.

These people are truly serious people whose pursuit for perfection is often a blessing and a vice to people around them.

The Good

The reformer's holy idea of perfection is omnipresent. Their greatest desire is to create goodness, maintain impeccable integrity in their dealings and to balance the chaos around them.

They are always the first to take the right action, standing up for what they believe in and acting upon it when others are meandering and compromising or lacking in courage, you can always count on a reformer to step up first and do what needs to be done.

They are also the best people when it comes to fixing things. You don't have to do many things around the house because their delight is in fixing things, moving furniture, adding value and creating something different or better.

The Bad

Living with these people is like a personal hell. You don't need to die to experience hell – all you need to do is to marry one or live in the same house with them as they constantly expect you to abide by the (or their) rules.

They also have an ultra strong tendency to lean towards hypocrisy because no one is perfect even if they set the standards. Hypercriticism makes being around them unbearable at times because they will always find fault with others and fix them.

Their most commonly displayed emotion is one of anger because nothing around them seems good enough to them – constantly resenting imperfection in things, circumstances or others.

How To Deal With Them

Because of their holy idea of perfection, their basic fear and tendency is to fall into sin/evil and become corrupt due to their own natural greed.

A self-preserving reformer must never be questioned about their personal reformative motives as they tend to keep to themselves about their grand plans for transforming the world. They do things quietly so the best way to deal with them is to acknowledge their efforts in little ways (they seldom show contentment or satisfaction)

A sexual reformer is one that needs constant attention to their plans. You have to be patient as you listen to them because they want to change the world so badly but they got no one to share them with. They tend to be lonely when no one acknowledges their grand plans.

A social reformer is one who often winds up like politicians and social activists. You have to put them with the right crowd for the wrong crowd will only reinforce their hypocrisy and turn the social reformer into a cult leader.

They work very well with enthusiasts (type 7) who are often sold and excited about their plans for reformation and they hate being around individualists (type 4) who are self indulgent, often depressed and doesn't get anything done.

Helpers live to serve. As long as they feel that they are in contribution to others, they feel they are worthy. A being of selflessness, they believe that giving to others is their highest calling as they feel that love is the most important emotion in the world.

These are the warmest, most helpful people around who will never forget your birthday (or feel really guilty when they do so...) and will go the extra mile to help one in need.

An extrovert in nature, they work hard to relate and show love to all their friends and family. They live for appreciation and often falls into the trap of tending to the needs of others at the neglect of their own which often causes a problem.

The Good

Helpers love the unbounded feeling of freedom which includes freedom of expressive their love to the world. An expressive being on unconditional love, they long to give and give and give until they can give no more.

Helpers are highly altruistic – you can always count on them to sacrifice themselves for the good of others, often at their own expense.

Being around them is good because they will always be there to fulfill your needs and feel their love.

The Bad

The problem with helpers is that they have a strong tendency to seek vainglory because of their love to help others. Because they feel that being in contribution to others is their greatest calling, they will do whatever it takes, even to the point of manipulation in order to get people to acknowledge their helpfulness. They are prone to flattery.

Some helpers, ironically... even though they are filled with love, can turn really ugly if their love is not reciprocated. They feel that they are heroes because of the loving and helping nature, they will constantly have a sense of entitlement to those closest to them – often feeling that people owe them appreciation and gratitude.

When their emotional needs go unmet, they come really bossy and manipulative because they have earned their right for reciprocation. At the worst case scenario, they might become hysterical, unreasonable, very difficult to deal with and even abusive!

How To Deal With Them

The best thing a helper can do for themselves is to take care of their own needs even when they feel full on in helping others. As long as they are kept from burnout, they are less susceptible to emotional exhaustion and dryness. They often fear that they are unworthy for others to love them.

A self preserving helper will help others and often refuse to tell others about their own needs. To help these people, you have to help them back behind the background otherwise they will feel that you are intruding their self-worth without realize that they are running on an empty fuel tank.

A sexual helper will need lots of love and care expressed visibly or visually. They must be acknowledged by their mates or they will malfunction. Be patient when listening to their meandering needs for acknowledgement and help them to help themselves and you'll do fine.

Social helpers are good in charitable organizations or counseling centers. Giving them good social projects is okay as long as the people they are serving give lots of encouragement and support. Take care of their needs when you see that they are serving too many people lest they feel burnt out with the huge burden or trying to please everyone.

They work very well with individualists (type 7) who are often deeply complex and have many different needs (which helpers love to be around and help them) and they hate being around challengers (type 8) who threaten their comfort zones.

Chapter 3:

The Achiever and The Individualist

Synopsis

Top achievers of the society, they live to achieve and achieve, they must! These people are never content with mediocrity and they will do whatever it takes to sing the song of victory!

This chapter talks about:

- What an achiever is all about

- Why are achiever good to have around

- What is most difficult about achievers

- Dealing with them and bringing out the best

- Who they get along with

- Who they don't along with

Championing the cause of accomplishment, loving an achiever for his or her high standards is the key to understanding these individuals. Just don't take their glory moments away from them and they will shine like a shooting star reaching greater heights!

"I am me. There is no one else like me." This is the cry of an individualist – one who is different and distinct from the rest (according to them...)

This chapter talks about:

- ➢ What an individualist is all about

- ➢ Why are individualist are good to have around

- ➢ What is most difficult about individualists

- ➢ Dealing with them and bringing out the best

- ➢ Who they get along with

- ➢ Who they don't along with

Elitist of society, they are always striving to be unique and different. Understanding them takes effort, but will yield their unique blend of humanity. Just don't ever remind them how 'common' they are.

The Next Two

Achievers are beings who live for validation. They will do whatever it takes to attain success, wealth, fame, or anything that will get the attention of their community.

They are the types that are hardworking, competitive, striving and loves high performance challenges and rewards such as top sales, best division or even the highest score in a video game.

They are also extroverted, have high energy because of the way they present themselves, love their images of success and will never back down lest they be labeled as a 'loser'.

The Good

An achiever lives for the goal – or the hope of attaining one. Because of their basic desire to appear that they are of value to themselves, others and society, they will strive for the results at all costs.

The best thing about them is that they strive for truthfulness – incredibly straightforward, they will cut to the chase or cut through all the smokescreens to get down to the truth whether in life, health, religion or any other matter.

Driven, self-confident and highly practical, their energy inspires people around them to work harder and they will rise through the ranks as they are good networkers as well.

The Bad

The worst thing about a person in this state is that find it hard to be intimate with other people.

They fixation on looking 'good' makes it hard for them to be authentically vulnerable which can be frustrating for partners.

Deep down inside, they are shameful for not being 'good enough' to others – which will often lead them into creating a false image that isn't true to themselves.

Achievers are fixated on vanity – often pleasing everybody in order to maintain their image and are prone to being deceitful.

How To Deal With Them

In order to get along with an achiever, you must help them to remove their basic fear of worthlessness – constantly reminding them that they are basically of value to everyone.

Self-preserving achievers are typically lonely achieving types because they won't share their weaknesses so you will need to fill in for them when you know they are lacking but not letting them know what you did because they don't want to appear in need.

Sexual achievers must have understanding partners who validate their self worth all the time by acknowledging their success, whether big or small. It is very important to realize that they want to appear successful and giving/providing to their mates as that is a sense of their achievement.

Social achievers must be acknowledged in public. Whether by winning competitions or high performance situations, be their support to see them win.

Make sure they do not let others see them when they lose.

They work very well with loyalists (type 6) who are loyal to them and feeds their ego of success and they hate being around peacemakers (type 9) who prefer giving in to mediocrity over shaking the norm of people in order to strive for excellence or success.

Themed as 'specials', the individualist is a person who thrives as being completely unique to the rest of humanity. They are very self-conscious about their individuality and are beings of boundless creativity because they are different from others.

Deep thinkers and analyzers, they are the philosophers of life and they have a strong interest in arts, even if they do not wind up to become artists.

They are aesthetically sensitive and they love everything about self-expression, self-discovery or self-revelation... often sharing their great findings to others and giving a strong contribution to the world.

The Good

Because they view themselves as inherently unique, they are often people who tend to think out of the box.

They love to return to the holy idea of origin – often going deep down into themselves to find the true 'source' and share that level of humanity with other people.

They are often very calm or level headed people – giving a poise of self control as they handle situations.

Their most powerful trait is that they value uniqueness, acknowledging the rarity found in others and are beings striving to be as genuine and authentic as possible. You can always count on them to express their true feelings without wearing a mask.

The Bad

An individualist normally has a strong tendency to be an elitist – disgusted by the commonness of the masses, they can become incredibly racist, prejudice and impatient towards differences, especially when it threatens their uniqueness and ideas.

They are also filled with envy – especially of things that they want so deeply that sets them apart from the rest.

When things go wrong in life for an individualist, they become hyper-analytical, often falling into deep bouts of depression and sadness. Withdrawal from the world and self-inflicted punishment (almost bordering to the point of masochism...) helps them to feel sane.

How To Deal With Them

Dealing with an individualist is simple. Because they value their uniqueness so deeply that they often view it as a blessing or a curse, it is okay to let them wallow in depression for awhile because they are emotionally complex and highly sensitive.

A self preserving individualist must be dealt with gently. Because their uniqueness is never shared with the rest of the world, one must learn to tolerate their tendency to become self-absorbed in deep thinking until they are ready to come out and live their lives.

A sexual individualist longs to share their authentic and unique self with their partners – often malfunctioning greatly when they are in (or after) an argument with their loved ones. If they are facing depressing, note that it is important not to yank them out of their shell because it will only further frustrate their depression.

Social individualists loves communal sharing and they love to share themselves authentically with large groups whom they feel that they are aloof their commonness. If things go wrong, they will often withdraw themselves seeing the world as cruel and long for a savior to come and rescue them.

At the end of the day, deep emotional understanding is important because all sub-types of the individualist long to be understood and accepted for who they truly are.

They find comfort with reformers (type 1) whose reforming ways gives them a channel that they can channel their unique and uncommon ways and they hate being around helpers (type 2) who probably don't understand their uniqueness and hates owing them a sense of entitlement (preferring withdrawal in depression).

Chapter 4:

The Investigator and The Loyalist

Synopsis

Whether they are Sherlock Holmes is besides the point. These people are the elite thinkers of society – you can always count on them to give you a deep analysis on a subject!

This chapter talks about:

- What an investigator is all about

- Why are investigators good to have around

- What is most difficult about investigators

- Dealing with them and bringing out the best

- Who they get along with

- Who they don't along with

Their quest for knowledge is admirable! Thank God for investigators, otherwise our world will be void of detailed knowledge!

They will stand by you till death. Such is the ideal of a loyalist – if you earn their trust, that is...

This chapter talks about:

> What a loyalist is all about

> Why are loyalists good to have around

> What is most difficult about loyalists

> Dealing with them and bringing out the best

> Who they get along with

> Who they don't along with

Championing the cause of loyalty, come what may... they WILL stay! – learn to love them, accept them for who they are and bring the best out of them!

2 More

An investigator, is a type of thinker who likes to take a back seat, observe the situation, make all the analytical considerations for the best options and comes back after a full analysis of the situation is done.

They typically do not share their emotional state with others as they hold back often finding security in their minds where they can withdraw and strategize, only to emerge later with full confidence!

You can always count on them to give intelligent answers, and when they are interested in something, they tend to become really well read and knowledgeable in that area.

They are also a little shy but more independent (or reluctant to accept help) preferring to get things done on their own even when other people are more than willing to give help.

The Good

To the investigator, knowledge conquers all – because their holy idea is based on omniscience. Their basic desire is to be competent in all that they endeavor, feeling ahead in terms of knowledge and understanding.

They are good at emotionally detaching themselves when it comes to handling mentally challenging tasks, undergoing large amounts of study and research till no ends – great if you really want to get down into detail over a complex subject.

The Bad

Investigators tend to be over analytical – hence the term... paralysis by analysis.

They are often very stingy people as well, not willing to share beyond their boundaries of safety and comfort. Because of their 'know-all' attitude, they tend to be aloof others often becoming very self-righteous and judgmental thinking that other people will never understand or know better.

At times, their quest for knowledge and understanding will make them highly covetous and greedy for more deep down. Their 'thirst' will never be satisfied and the worst part is, they do not emotionally express this.

How To Deal With Them

Deep down inside, investigators are sensitive people and really restraint when it comes to emotional expression.

When dealing with self-preservation investigators, do not inquire about their secret thoughts or deep research. They will feel that you will not understand them anyway and it is highly intrusive of their privacy.

When dealing with sexual investigators, it can be a very complex communication process indeed. One reason is because they are not very good at communicating their inner feelings, yet they long to share their understanding on certain topics to their partners deeply. The best thing you can do is to try and meet them half way and research on the topic well enough to have an intelligent conversation with them.

Last but not least are the social investigators – the crowd will have to tolerate with their social arrogance, having to put up to their long theories (and sometimes tiresome, boring ones) but try and appear interested long enough to give them acknowledgement of their great understanding and you'll do fine with them.

They work very well with challengers (type 8) who are often pushes them to push their boundaries of omniscience and they hate being around enthusiasts (type 7) whose sanguine nature turns off the melancholic investigators with their mindless fun and excitement.

A loyalist is a person who is epitomized by the famous song "Stand by me". The day they build solid trust with someone, they will stick by them all the way until the end.

They are a very unique type of people when it comes to trust because they tend to trust people almost as much as they distrust people at the same time. These people are always constantly looking for something or someone to believe in deeply – once the people they believe in have 'earned their trust', they will be loyal till death.

The Good

The good thing about loyalists is that they are really courageous towards people who've earned their trust – often metaphorically throwing themselves in front of traffic to save them.

Deep down inside, they want to feel safe – they want to believe that in a loyal, trusting relationship, there is no fear of betrayal and will often project these to their trusted people, especially their life partners. They make very good life partners at the same time too.

Having a holy idea of faith, they constantly believe that miracles will happen and even though the people they trust do screw up, they will have the tendency to believe in them until they become a better person.

The Bad

Loyalists are sometimes cowards – feeling insecure with people around them.

They are so conflicted with trust and distrust that it will appear really conflicting at times (until the person earns their trust).

They are also phobic beings – afraid of a lot of things. While they may be good at fixing problems, they are also filled with anxiety to the core as they don't really have peace of mind.

How To Deal With Them

Since loyalists are generally afraid of isolation and vulnerability, the best way is to always calm them down and comfort them – showing them that you too can be trustworthy because deep down inside, they are always suspicious of others (hence their fixation on lots and lots of loyalty).

A self-preserving loyalist will always be working alone, quietly helping others fearful of people discovering their lack in their being.

The best way to deal with them is to return their trust and give them faith.

A sexual loyalist will always stick to the mate, but sometimes, being loyal for the wrong things is always bad – so focus on growing them instead.

Last but not least, a social loyalist is a person who will always stick with a group or a cause all the way till the end.

They work very well with peacemakers (type 9) who are often reinforces their loyalist and safe seeking nature and they hate being around achievers (type 3) who gives them a feeling of insecurity as it shakes their comfort zone of safety at the same time.

Chapter 5:

Synopsis

The life of the party and the ever omnipresent voice of excitement – you have got to love them for their multitalented, multifaceted nature.

This chapter talks about:

> What an enthusiast is all about

> Why are enthusiasts good to have around

> What is most difficult about enthusiasts

> Dealing with them and bringing out the best

> Who they get along with

> Who they don't along with

They get bored easily and may speed ahead without you. Are you up to the challenge on keeping up with an enthusiast? Let's race!

They will be the person shouting in your ear or they may be someone who will push you to greater heights. Such is the role of a challenger who will never back down on a fight... or let you back down from one!

This chapter talks about:

> What a challenger is all about

> Why are challengers good to have around

> What is most difficult about challengers

> Dealing with them and bringing out the best

> Who they get along with

> Who they don't along with

Their anger is a force to be reckoned with! But they will always be the strong one. You got to love them because of their strengths for without them, no one will get anything done...

Love. Peace. Serenity. Stillness. Peace lovers. Shhhh... keep the quietness otherwise it will shake them up!

This chapter talks about:

> What a peacemaker is all about

> Why are peacemakers good to have around

> What is most difficult about peacemakers

> Dealing with them and bringing out the best

> Who they get along with

> Who they don't along with

Like a firm rock, they will not be moved, yet they are the most loving friends to have around! Learn to love them, cherish them and feel the serenity around them! Truly a good friend to have indeed!

The Last 3

The enthusiast is an exciting person to be around with. They are always constantly seeking excitement, pleasure and a way to distract them from the mundane everyday life.

They are constantly living in a bright future – anticipating the fun and excitement that will come out of it and can't wait to get there, bring the fun and excitement with other people along.

They are creative, multi talented and open minded. They are also unbridled and deny any form of self-denial or delayed gratification.

Natural born promoters, they often do not focus on one thing for long and moves on to the next most exciting thing. They especially love the spotlight being shined upon them.

The Good

These enthusiasts love doing stuff – anything that engages their senses full on really turns them on... even the thought of doing it later! This is a very good motivating factor when they need to rile up a dead group of people who are emotionally dull. There's never a dull moment with enthusiasts around.

Their zeal to experience life is huge – often engaging themselves 100% in a task to feel it to the maximum. Such a kind of enthusiasm of life is so contagious that it even inspires other people!

They are also very practical people who have lots of skills and love to do all kinds of things.

The Bad

The sad thing about enthusiasts is that their attention span is like a flash in a pan. The moment they get bored, they will abandon the project.

They get bored really easily because they hate that the most. They also have the temptation of moving too fast, often abandoning the things they are supposed to do in the process or spreading themselves too thinly.

Their biggest vice is that they want everything – everything they set their eyes on in the worst form of gluttony.

The worst part is, their self centered nature gives them a great deal of entitlement (of fun perhaps…) and they have a hard time focusing on other people because of that.

How To Deal With Them

Self-preserving enthusiasts will do whatever they feel is fun (an example would be indulging in video games for prolonged hours). The only way to distract them from the fun is to give them something else more fun because they will not tell you why they like something.

Sexual enthusiasts must be with exciting partners – perhaps traveling the world or engaging in constant fun activities. If you keep him or her at home, it will be a relationship suicide.

The social type will like to go to a lot of parties often or be in the limelight for challenges – this will make them feel whole.

They work very well with investigators (type 5) because they will do all the thinking for them (and attend to details when they plan to do something fun...) and they hate being around reformers (type 1) who they believe are fun killers.

 A challenger doesn't want to be controlled. Full stop.

They consider themselves and only themselves to be the master of their own fate – having full autonomy to live their lives. Extremely tough minded people, they will keep on pushing themselves to great extremes in order to get the best results even if they are only challenging themselves.

Since their instincts are so strong, they often have strong physical appetites to get exactly whatever result they want out from life. Often they also hate working for others, choosing to work for themselves.

They are also people who tend to be financially independent or capable. They don't like people to see them as a weak person.

The Good

Highly noble and upright, they will do whatever it takes to show themselves as the source of strength and protect the weak. You can definitely count on them to get things done easily – often without relying on the help of others.

Having the holy idea of truth, they will never surrender or compromise even under temptation to get something in exchange for falsehood.

These people are not petty – they will show their strengths and will not be concerned for the pettiness of those weaker than them in terms of what they think about him because he or she will always want to appear to be a magnanimous to others.

The Bad

Challengers get angry easily and will easily take revenge on someone who wrongs them.

In other words, their form of vengeance can often include working harder to prove them wrong, make more money to hide their weakness, counter their falsehood or just become stronger.

They fear loss of control so greatly that they become tyrants in the process. Lust for all things is common for the challenger because of strong cravings and desires.

How To Deal With Them

Self preserving challenges live in their own personal battlefield where their greatest enemy to challenge is always themselves. Don't ask them why they want to challenge anything – they will do it regardless of whatever people think and we can only let them grow when they get more results.

Sexual challengers are very difficult to live with because they either always want to challenge or change their partners or they will vent out lots of frustration against weaker people to their mates. A mate must be very strong and have huge emotional reservoirs – showing lots of patience at the same time.

Social challengers will sometimes challenge people on a higher level or in public. Don't get into a fight with them because they will have no problems fighting (even physically) in broad daylight.

They work very well with helpers (type 2) because they like people helping them and they hate being around investigators (type 5) who they think are too slow to get anything done with their overly analytical attitudes.

Peacemakers love peace of course – and they will do whatever it takes to maintain it at all costs. Incredibly introverted, they often seen laid back, as though they are not fully present in whatever they are engaged in.

They tend to be very optimistic in life believing that somehow, everything will work out in the end whatever may come. They make very warm and attentive friends.

Because they are afraid of conflict, they often are resistant to any forms of changes that will bring up these unpleasant feelings of tension. They are less hesitant to express their anger outwardly compared to the challenger or the reformer.

The Good

Because they are such loving, supportive people, they tend to make the best parents or become your warmest friends whenever you need someone to talk to.

Never hot headed, their supportive nature brings a sense of calmness and peace to all around them. Their laid back nature dissolves any feelings of unpleasantness compared to other confrontational types. They are people of serenity.

You get a lot of peace of mind by just being around them.

The Bad

It is almost impossible to coerce these people against their will as they often turn out to be one of the most stubborn people around. Indolent and unmoving, they tend to forget about themselves.

Deep down inside, they don't like to be bossed around and on the surface, they might appear to be pleasing and compliant, giving in to your every demand, they are actually harboring a deep seated grudge that when accumulated over a long time, will result in explosive rage or passive-aggressive behavioral manifestations.

Sometimes, they are too easy going and they don't have a care in the world.

Their tendency to overlook conflict can also have an adverse effect on human relations, especially during the times when results affect the most.

How To Deal With Them

Don't boss them around. Let them know that the best peace and harmony they can get with other people is to make the choices that best support this.

Self-preserving peacemakers may seem very disconnected, but just do what you can to support their peaceful surroundings.

Sexual peacemakers love the intimacy of a calm and serene relationship and try not to cause conflict with them which will cause them to clam up completely.

Social peacemakers are a very interesting type. They like being around people that give them a community and a sense of peacefulness – serving and pleasing others. Putting these type of people in a non-intrusive, safe environment helps them to be themselves. That way, it will subdue their fear of feeling losing something or being annihilated.

They work very well with achievers (type 3) because they like who will motivate them and sell them a beautiful dream and they hate being around loyalists (type 6) who they think are different from the way they think about people.

Chapter 6:

Personalities

Synopsis

We are all different! You know you do not have to be a rocket scientist to know this. However, when it comes to dealing with the people who do not have the same personality like yours, how would you react?

Different People

Just because you have been a joker, it does not mean you can make a CEO of a multi-national company laughs. Just because you are passionate about people, it does not mean your boss thinks the same way like you do. Just because you do not want to hurt your best friend, it does not mean you should withhold the unpleasant information (being cheated by the boyfriend) from her.

When I was working in a jewelry company, I had no idea what was wrong with my boss that he kept pushing the limit of his employers to work overtime. When that happened, some of the staffs start mumbling and complaining about not having enough time to spend with their families or loved ones. To these staffs, relationships with their loved ones mean a lot to them.

On the other hand, my boss had a totally different idea about the entire incident. There was only one thing in his mind – delivering the promise, best products and excellent service to his big client. It is not difficult to understand why he kept pushing the staffs to the limit. No matter what it takes, his priority to keep his business staying at the top in the industry.

It took me a while to understand this.

In this e-book, you will learn and understand much more about the different types of personalities. While everyone is unique, you can generally group them into 9 types: Controller, promoter, analyzer, supporter, controller/analyzer, promoter/controller, promoter supporter, supporter analyzer and centric.

Don't worry if you do not know what these terms mean. As you journey together with this e-book, you are going to get acquainted with these personalities and your benefit?

Understand them better and know how to deal with them effectively.

Each personality type will be discussed in their areas of attributes, strengths, weaknesses and the right way to deal with them.

Chapter 7:

The Controller, Promoter and Analyzer

Synopsis

Do you have what it takes to be a controller? What does it mean to have the controller mindset and conduct? Don't be scared by the term of controller. As you learn their attributes in this chapter, you are going to be equipped to deal with them effectively.

This chapter talks about:

- ➢ The Attributes of the Controller Personality
- ➢ How to Deal With a Controller?

Not all of us like the terms of controllers but you will learn exactly why you need these controllers on earth to make the world a better place to be.

Have you got friends who are extremely expressive? They will shout all of a sudden, and they tend to be the most creative persons you could possibly find on earth. They are the promoters!

This chapter talks about:

- ➢ The Attributes of the Promoter Personality

- ➢ How to Deal With a Promoter?

It is usually fun to have a promoter in the group because they are the ones who entertain us the most. Sounds good, but this will also mean some people are going to be irritated simply because of their expressive actions.

Have you ever met someone who throws a million questions before he steps his foot on a boat? If you haven't but you have faced the similar scenario above, you have just had your experience with an analyzer.

This chapter talks about:

> The Attributes of the Analyzer Personality

> How to Deal With an Analyzer?

Analyzers are usually slow and secure. You will learn exactly why from the information I am going to share with you starting from the next page.

The First 3

A controller is usually someone who takes initiative in doing things naturally. They are the ones who have no problems with decision making. These people appear to be strong-willed, confident, capable and efficient.

When controllers are hanging out with their friends, they will come out with ideas of the activities. They will decide where the places will be and who will be in-charge of a certain task. When a controller is running his own company, he knows exactly which direction to head to. In a family, if a husband is a controller, the wife and children will not need to worry about a thing simply because the husband has already made all the decisions.

This group of people is very task-oriented. Whenever a task is given to them, you can be sure they are in good hands and know they will get it done on time. Their motto is this – no matter what it takes, it has to be done.

How about the sensitive side of them? Well, if you are a lady and looking for a new age sensitive guy, controllers are going to disappoint you.

Controllers appear to be insensitive and emotions will not normally affect them in any way. While some of your friends may not even dare to confront you of your wrongdoings, these people have no problems with it comes to confrontation.

There are tons of ways, really but for the purpose of this e-book, I will share few practical points so that you can use them in time of need.

Be Submissive: Submission basically means to obey and do what your superior asks you to do (within the legal boundaries). Digging deeper, submission is more than just obedience and conduct. If you think about it, submission comes when there is disagreement. Even when there are times you do not agree with your boss' idea, you will still have to submit to him. If you never know, bosses favor those subordinates who submit to them rather than those who are against them.

Know What Is Best For Them: This can be easier for you now as you already know what they have in mind already – results. So whenever you work with them, you must work for their best interests.

I know we mentioned about submission in the previous points but will it be possible for your boss to implement the ideas you have in mind? The answer is a very resounding yes! It is when your idea is perceived to be much more workable, effective and practical than your boss' idea.

When he knows your ideas will help him to achieve the goals (which is to make bucket loads of money, branding or involves in charity) of the company, he will have no problems saying 'yes' to your proposed ideas. It is simply for the good of the company.

Many people on earth out there find it difficult to work with or for those who have the controller personality. Well, things change when you know what they think and what matters to them. When you do, unity and harmony sets in.

Have you ever wondered why some of your colleagues gain favors from your superiors? They just know how to make their bosses happy. Even though most of the examples above are illustrated in the context of an employment, you will find controllers among your friends and family as well. I believe you are able to identify them from now on.

Although controllers are the ones who make decisions for the group or organizations, they may not be the ones who get the most attention at the time. The moment the planning part is done, the controllers' job is also done.

On the other hand, promoter may capture the attention of the public very easily simply because of their promoting nature. They are expressive, keep the crowd entertained, come out with the jokes spontaneously and capture the attention of the people who are present. The things that they say do not even need to make sense.

They appear to be happy, active, outgoing and friendly. Some may even wonder why they can talk and express so well and at the same time, a minority will find him irritating. People generally love to have promoters around because they are not boring and personable.

Who are the examples of a promoter?

- The Mask (acted by Jim Carrey)
- Buddy Love from the Nutty Professor Movie
- Shrek's Donkey

Yeah I know they are all fictional characters but I am sure you are able to tell who have got the promoter's attributes among the people around you.

There is always a way to tame the monkey, if you know how. Well, perhaps not so much of taming them but if you know the tricks, it is going to help you to get along with the promoters pretty well. By 'pretty well', I mean the moment can be shared and enjoyed by the both parties.

Provide Solution to Them: You would not want to hand the job over to an impulsive person when it comes to problem solving. Promoters may not be the best source to solve problems, they are definitely great help when it comes to implementation of the plan. You will be amazed with how fun the journey can be with the promoters around.

They Want Recognition: The best way to motivate promoters is to give them recognition. They love to be recognized of the contribution they have invested. For instance, if you compliment Dennis (a promoter) for doing a great job in front of the crowd, he is going to remember this for a long time and the best part is, he will want to work with you again and again.

Protect Their Ego: Be extra careful when dealing with them. They are super sensitive with their ego and you have got to try your very best to protect their ego. The best place to confront them is usually when nobody else is around. Do it sincerely and honestly.

Share Interpersonal Feelings with Them: If you can find ways to have a heart to heart talk to them, it will be great. Even most of them are jokes, they also enjoy this kind of deep conversation with their peers. Even though they are always expressive, they know what to let out and what not. Hence, your secrets are always safe with them.

The bottom line is this. Promoters must be allowed space to express themselves. Sometimes they are very difficult to understand and nevertheless, they make the journey much more fun and enjoyable. Eliminate essential decision making process from them. They are not born for it. However, involve them in the implementation and they will make it a pleasant one.

The analyzers are very feeling-based. Most of the time, they make decision based on their feelings on security. If there is any sense of insecurity, the process will take even longer, simply because they need to gather more data for themselves or the situations.

Data and analysis are extremely important to this group of people. When problem arises, they will take time to study, gather data and analyze the situation with whatever resources available. Not only data and facts, opinions and thoughts of the people involved are also essential to them.

Normally analyzers appear to be very academic and tend to be very serious when it comes to working environment. Their conversation maybe based on facts, histories or past illustrations.

Some people may find talking to them boring and at the same time, things that are coming out from their mouth are good to be used for advice.

One of the common examples would include middle-aged staffs that have little interests in the culture change, especially in the company. They are comfortable with where they currently are and risk is just not something they would want on their way. They can be secure yet stubborn.

Dealing with an analyzer may require some skills. Always remember, all they want is just security and data. When you have these two things with you, you can't go wrong with an analyzer.

Here are a few more practical ways...

Use Their Ability to Build Friendship: In case you do not know, analyzers tend to use their ability to gain attention or build friendship, rather than their genuine self. If you can provide an environment to meet friends or build relationships with others through their ability (probably working on a big project together), things are going to be better for them.

Encourage Them to be Less Critical: Yes, they are critical definitely but you can also ease their critics by assuring them it is time to implement the strategies and there is no need to worry about the errors that are going to happen. Spend more effort to convince and encourage them.

Tell Them Things That They Do Not Know: Especially when you are in the meeting, things that they already know will only irritate them if you repeat. When you provide them the useful information which they need to help in solving the problems, you will gain their favor easily.

Those are the attributes of an analyzer and I can't stress this point enough – it is all about security and data.

Chapter 8:
The Supporter, Promoter/Supporter and Promoter/Controller

Synopsis

You have probably seen supporters all around you. When you are emotionally weak, they are usually the ones you would want to go to. They are the people person and we call them the supporters.

This chapter talks about:

> The Attributes of the Supporter Personality

> How to Deal With a Supporter?

Not only there are promoters and supporters on earth. Some people have the mixed personality that comes with promoter as well as supporters. We call it the promoter/supporter personality.
This chapter talks about:

> The Attributes of the Promoter/Supporter Personality

> How to Deal With a Promoter/Supporter?

Have you seen people who have been bragging about their own success and no joke, they are really successful? This is one of the examples of promoter/controller.

This chapter talks about:

- ➢ The Attributes of the Promoter/Controller Personality

- ➢ How to Deal With a Promoter/Controller?

The Next 3

Supporters are usually likable and very people-oriented. For promoters, people enjoy a promoter's presence solely because of his ability to entertain. However, people place their trusts on the supporters mainly because of their ability to care, encourage and support.

This is why, when you break up with your boyfriend of 10 years, you wouldn't want to go to a controller or analyzer, but a supporter for comfort.

Since it is their nature to be people-oriented, they tend to avoid personal conflicts in any way possible; even it means to cost the innocence of themselves. It will be really difficult for them to reject people and they will please anyone who comes on their ways (and of course, I am not talking about the criminal kind of demand).

They are also very responsive to people. When people are around, they will usually blend in to the conversation and go with the flow. They let others to initiate any kinds of activities and yet they do not have the interest to impress others.

This is the species that appear to be harmless and non-threatening. Even when they are threatened, they will not make it to the public and some of them suppress their feelings to the point of depression, which is not good at all.

Thus far, supporters appear to be the nice and easy kind of person to go to. In fact, it is dangerous to have this kind of mindset because supporters also appear to be a time bomb which does not give you an idea when it is going to explode.

Why is that?

The burdens they carry for others may become a heavy and it is not uncommon to find the nicest person who always listens to you and pleases you has depression. This may even be the case without any of our acknowledgement.

Don't Push Them Too Hard: Now that you know they will say 'yes' to almost anything you ask of them and it is not a good idea to push them to the limit and take them for granted. Remember, they are human beings too.

Be Grateful to Them: Even though recognition or rewards may not be the things they are looking for, it would be nice to give them encouragement and a pat on their shoulder for the things they have done for you. Remember the times when he was there when you were totally down? This is how you can payback.

Help Them to Stand Up For Themselves: I know it is abnormal for the supporters to express what is in their hearts but nevertheless you can encourage them to do so. They have the rights to voice out their opinions too. Since it is not nature to them, you can push them a little bit to protect themselves in the future.

Now that you know the reasons behind the supporters are being emotional and people-oriented. Just bear in your mind when you are dealing with them you need to acknowledge them for what they have done for courtesy's sake and never ever take them for granted.

Basically, the promoter/supporter personality is the mixture of promoter and supporter personalities. A promoter may be fun to hang out with but it does not mean he has genuine friendships at all. The same goes to a supporter – one does not need to capture the attention of the crowd in order to have a lot of genuine friendships.

What happens to the promoter/supporter personality then? It is simply referring to a person who is very expressive in things that he does and at the same time, he values the relationships and people around him.

This kind of people uses their charisma to build relationships with the people around him. Even though they appear to be the star in the crowd, relationships with people is definitely a big thing to him.

While promoters may only value their own opinions, in the promoter/supporter personality, a person values both his own and the ideas of others. This kind of people can be more appealing simply because of the hidden strength they have.

I would say the promoter/supporter personality is in those who like to hang out without much seriousness in a tensed environment. Artists, designers, freelancers or clowns may have this kind of personality.

How do you deal with them, then?

Esteem Them in Public: You need to esteem them in the public for the things they have done and contributed. They enjoyed being recognized and nevertheless they are also the supporters. They must have helped the people around them in one way or another.

Let Them Develop Genuine Friendships: Even though they appear to be charismatic, I suppose they are afraid of being lonely. This is probably one of the hidden secrets that come with the promoter/supporter.

Work Best in a Group: In case you are to assign them to work, let them work in a group. They love to laugh and at the same time, they love people. Working in a group can help them to develop close relationships with his peers and in turn this will also make the workplace a great place to be.

Now that you have met the promoter/supporter, can you identify any of your friends who belong to this group?

A person with promoter/controller personality is normally expressive in an aggressive way. Unlike promoter/supporter, relationships may not matter to them but success and sense of achievement can be a really big thing to them.

Now, a controller may be achieving great success but still remains a low profile. I personally know a person who has been declared bankruptcy and yet he owns a company that makes millions of dollars in profit yearly. On the other hand, promoter/controller can be achieving great success at the same time, but the fact that he is rich and successful is made known to all over the world.

This group of people love challenges and always strives to win. Not just to win, but to win with flying colors. It is not quite common for them to stay in the same position for long. They need to jump from one place to another. Stagnancy will just bore them and they chase their goals and dreams with intensity.

In terms of conversations, they are the ones who dominate. People listen to them the moment they speak and their voices turn out to be clearly visible. In addition, speeches that they make will usually carry much weight.

Probably by now, you would not want to work under a boss who has a promoter/controller personality. Or perhaps, you want to be a promoter/controller. Either way is totally fine.

Here is how you can deal with them...

Contribute Ideas Based on Their Interests: If you are given a chance to contribute ideas to a promoter/controller, you must do it right. Not to mention you do not get many chances to speak to them, things that you say to them must contribute to help them achieve their goals and dreams.

Esteem Their Success: Yes, promoters/controllers can be very egoistic at times. One thing you can do to make them happy if to esteem their success. Celebrate their success and tell them that they have done a good job. If the compliment if given in front of a big crowd, it is even better. The surely want to be recognized of their success.

Involve Them to Work in Groups: If it is possible, try to get them to work in groups. Their pace of working may not be pleasant while working with the rest of the group members, but it is a good way to allow them to learn to journey together with the team, rather than just having to walk alone.

In short, promoters/controllers are the ones who get things done effectively with the intention of being recognized for their achievements. When you understand this, you know why they behave in such a way.

Chapter 9:

The Controller/Analyzer , Analyzer/Supporter and Centric

Synopsis

It is truly a combination of both controller and analyzer personalities. This kind of personality appears to be distant and people find it hard to gain access to their lives.

This chapter talks about:

> - The Attributes of the Controller/Analyzer Personality
> - How to Deal With a Controller/Analyzer?

Now you have a mixture of analyzer and supporter's personalities. We call them the analyzer/supporter personality.

This chapter talks about:

> - The Attributes of the Analyzer/Supporter Personality
> - How to Deal With a Analyzer/Supporter?

Do you believe there are people who have all of the personalities discussed in this e-book? These people have what we call the centric personality.

This chapter talks about:

- The Attributes of the Centric Personality
- How to Deal With a Centric?

3 More

The first thing that comes to my mind in relation to the controller/analyzer personality is this – they are stiff! I am not sure if it is the right word to describe them but to me, they are probably the last person on earth I would want to hang out with. Unless it is required, there will be no way I'd want to meet them.

Anyway, let's talk about the controllers/analyzers. They are efficient and business-minded. Apart from getting desired results, they are also keen in gathering information. Even sometimes the implementation of the plan may take much longer than required, nevertheless the probability of the success is almost guaranteed.

This group of people is not so good in placing their trusts on others. They can be very critical and judgmental to the point that they only place their trusts on the people who have been working effectively for them in the past. Any first timers will have to perform extremely well in order to gain the initial favor of the controllers/analyzers.

Needless to say, they are very task-oriented. They are not driven by emotions and often very rational when it comes to making decisions. They are calm and steady even the biggest obstacles set in. No matter what, they will get it done.

Finally, it is normal to them so scan through the situation or a person who is in front of them. They will generate all kinds of perceptions, data and judgment on the situations and person, causing the person especially to panic easily.

Controllers/analyzers appear to be serious and boring. How do you deal with them, then?

Provide Detailed Blueprint: Forget about telling them about Justin Bieber's concert is coming. They just want to know what you have to offer to help them achieve their goals and what are the steps they need to take to bring their goals to pass.

Extra Effort to Minimize Errors: When you are working with them, you need to pay careful attention to details and give more than 100% of your energy. You can't possibly allow any margins for errors and to controllers/analyzers, errors will cost them a lot of resources. So be careful.

Efficiency: All they want is efficiency. If you can make use of the resources available, you are getting their attention and they would want to involve you to work as a part of their team.

Although I personally find it difficult to deal with controllers/analyzers, I am not suggesting this is the case for everyone. I believe the world needs controllers/analyzers to direct and implement the strategies for making the world a better place for everyone.

The group of analyzers/supporters is rather interesting. Even relationships may matter to them, they will always struggle to develop genuine friendships simply because of their analyzer nature as well.

For instance, they may long for friendships and at the same time, they are also critical when it comes to choosing the right friends.

As a result, they rarely initiate conversations in interpersonal situations. They will usually wait for others to approach them or let others to voice out their opinions before they speak their very first word in the conversation.

They can be of very good support yet analytical. Time is needed for them to place their trust fully on a person.

Analyzers are usually slower before they make decisions on the matters. Hence, some of the best ways are to give them more space to develop friendships.

Make Use of Good Testimonials: When you are talking to an analyzer/supporter, they can easily take the things you said about another person to their hearts. So when the next time an analyzer/supporter meets the person you mentioned to him in the past, he will have a brief idea of how good or bad the person can be. He may either be defensive or open to the friendship, based on the testimonials you said. So you must be careful with the words you use to talk about other people in front of the analyzers/supporters.

Give Them More Space to Develop Friendship: Certain things in life just can't be forced. For the analyzers/supporters, even though they may long for sincere friendships, you need to give them more space to develop this kind of relationships.

Analyzers/Supporters can be understood easily when you know what is going on around them. Always remember, they are a bit slow when it comes to develop friendships so you just need to go with their pace.

Now, I would say the people with the centric personality are almost perfect. They use the right approach to communicate, depending on who they are talking to. When they are talking to controllers, they switch their mode to relate to the controllers. When people come to them for support, they become compassionate with the feelings of the broken-hearted.

Isn't it amazing if we have the centric personality?

Even they are strong-willed, they do not appear to be manipulative. Even when they are supporting, they do not try to withhold unpleasant information from the intended person. In fact, they choose the correct way to deliver the bad news to the person.

In the working environment, they can probably get along well with both superiors and also subordinates. Bosses love them and staffs are happy to work under them.

Seriously, they appear to be flawless and people with centric personality are usually the most charismatic leaders you could possibly find on earth.

Seriously, you just need to be yourself. Let the centric read your mind and do his wonders while talking to you. Of course, there are also certain things you can do to make them feel better. Here are some of them...

Honesty: Have you ever heard of the saying that goes, "Honesty is the best policy"? If you have been thinking to use the right approach and words to impress the centric, let me suggest that there will be no such need for it. They know exactly what you are thinking the moment they start talking to you. So just be honest to them.

Understand They Are Different at Times: Don't be surprised if you see the different sides of the centric. It is just in them. They can be expressive this hour, and they can be very controlling and analytic during meetings.

Learn from Them: If you are able to, please learn from them because the world need more people like them to help make the world an awesome place to be. If you are able to adapt some of their ways of handling things, you are going to be different!

Centric appears to have no character flaws but this is not true. Nobody is born perfect under the sun. The trick about centric is that, they just know how to play the game. So if you want to have a centric personality, this chapter is definitely here to help.

Chapter 10:

Synopsis

Becoming a light-worker or dark-worker isn't something that simply occurs. It's a witting choice, one the huge bulk of individuals never arrive at.

You might have leanings toward one polarity or the other, and you may certainly experiment with both polarities as much as you want, but becoming a light-worker or dark-worker signifies making a particular commitment to command of a single polarity.

Different Poles

When you choose to polarize, you're building a commitment to living a particular sort of life. It's like arriving at a commitment to a specific field that takes years to master, like preparation for the Olympic Games, becoming a musician, or becoming a chess master.

You aren't simply going to rouse one day to find that ... yup... you're a black belt, nor will you abruptly wake up and recognize you're a light-worker or a dark-worker. Polarizing as a light-worker or dark-worker is a vast long-term dedication. It doesn't simply occur by itself instantly from insight.

The determination to polarize is a determination you make with every fiber of your being. For a few individuals it might be an innate choice, felt as a sort of calling. Other people must spend much time exploring both polarities to make the polarization dedication really consciously and deliberately. But most individuals never polarize.

If you polarize as a light-worker, you're committing your life to assisting the greater good. If you polarize as a dark-worker, you're committing your life to assisting yourself.

It ought to be sort of obvious that most individuals never make this sort of commitment in their whole lives. Therefore, most individuals are neither lightworkers nor dark-workers. The 2 extremes of dedicating one's life to assisting the greater good or to assisting one's own self-concern are not attractive to most individuals. It's merely not for them.

Following polarizing, your polarity becomes the key focus of your life. You live and breathe it daily. It virtually gets to be part of your DNA. It's unimaginable to compartmentalize such a dedication. You can't work at a lowly job and do light-working or dark-working unofficially. That's like trying to be President of the United States "unofficially". Being a light-worker or dark-worker is a 24/7 thing, all year. It's who you are, not simply what you do.

Those who haven't polarized are free to feel both polarities, however at a much lower level of strength than either a light-worker or dark-worker may. As a matter of fact, it's of great advantage to explore both polarities and comprehend how they work.

If you're a light-worker or dark-worker, you'll have no question about it. That's by definition. If you've any question about it, you haven't polarized. This is as primary a matter as recognizing you're a black belt in a particular martial art. If you have to question, you're not a black belt.

The rationality for polarizing is because you're prepared to make a witting dedication to a particular sort of life. You're wishing to dedicate your whole being either to assisting the greater good or to assisting yourself. That dedication becomes your life intention. It becomes the very center of your identity. You're stating to the cosmos, "That's who I am."

When you make this dedication, you'll know yourself in a way you've never known yourself previously. You'll wake up daily recognizing why you're here, not because somebody told you why, but as you've specified your own why with the power of conscious choice. Each moment of each day, you'll recognize whom you are and what you're here to accomplish.

Polarization brings a fresh level of strength, drive, and motivation. Troubles and obstacles that previously would have overrun you will appear like pettiness. Once you set a goal that lines up with your polarity, you'll recognize — not wish – it will be achieved.

Acting replaces attempting. Therefore, you'll expand the scope of your goals to equal your strength. You'll likewise greatly expand your timeline for considering the outcomes of your choices, thinking ten, twenty, many years ahead as a foregone conclusion. Short-term follies will be substituted by long-term allegiances.

There are levels of polarization. The more polarized you get, the more you tap into your richest degrees of inner power. Whether you're a dark-worker or a light-worker, your origin of force is always found inside.

It isn't a sort of means or positional power. You may be deprived of all your worldly titles and possessions and yet feel even as secure. As a light-worker, your power flows outward. As a dark-worker, your power flows inward. The origin of this flow is always within you — based inside your consciousness — and your polarity regulates the flow's direction.

If you don't wish to polarize, don't. You're free to go along utilizing both polarities if you so decide. Simply be aware that you may never expect to surmount either polarity unless you dedicate to one or the other. Put differently, if you don't polarize, you'll forever live with the knowledge that you lived far beneath your potential in terms of your power to assist others or to assist yourself. Your assistance to the world as well as your assistance to yourself will be average at best compared to what you may have accomplished had you polarized. This ought to be sort of obvious. Once you polarize, you're making a solid dedication, and when you're really dedicated to something, you'll invest a lot more time and energy into your quests than you would differently.

Polarization is a particular sort of dedication, like dedicating to mastery of a particular field like music, artistry, medicine, or computer programming. Most individuals never make such a big dedication. But you can't hope to control anything unless you dedicate to mastery of one thing.

Control is a procedure, not a place. Control is when you turn a want into a downright must. For light-workers and dark workers, these dedications are attained for different reasons.

However, in either case, a witting conclusion is made to devote one's time, power, resources, and talents to the selected role with an elevated degree of intensity. That strength of focus is possibly what most distinguishes somebody who's polarized.

Wrapping Up

Now that you know who you are – it is time to live life authentically!

Don't beat yourself up because you don't like your 'type'. You are all you've got so treat your life with care. If you do not live it authentically, you will only be living a half cooked life because that is not who you are!

Enjoy the journey of self discover and share this with others!